The Laws of Wealth

How to Acquire, Keep and Enjoy Lasting Wealth

Jeff Davis

This book is dedicated to my wife and children. It is my love for them that prompted me to begin a journey to understand wealth. It is my desire for them to live a better life with me being in their lives that drives me to want to understand how to build and keep wealth.

I am thankful every day for being able to live a life that is full of purpose.

Jeff Davis

Being One with Yourself

Did you know the greatest enemy you have to your future success is someone you meet every morning. That's right. You see them often. You talk to them every day. And depending on how the conversation goes, you may be depressed by them each day.

Where do I meet them, you ask? When do I talk to them?

Every morning when you go into the bathroom, look into the mirror and greet yourself.

If you are not careful, you can become your own worst enemy. How, you ask? By talking down to yourself, talking bad about yourself and encouraging yourself in all of your faults.

Happiness is a state of mind; joy is a state of being. Happiness is based on your interpretation of your circumstances. It's not what happens to you. It's how you perceive things inside of you that determine if your life will lift you up or tear you down.

Everyone has problems. We all deal with situations and difficulties that are hard on us. The challenge is not the problem; what's even more important is how we internalize the problem. What do we tell ourselves about the situation we are facing.

You are driving in your car. You are cruising along at 65 miles an hour when you hear an explosion. Your tire blows out and you move to the side of the road. It's getting late and you feel bad. You begin to talk to yourself and curse yourself for not seeing this happening earlier. You tell yourself you should have checked the tire. You beat yourself up.

Is that you? Or do you see it as "things happen, it's not always someone else's fault and I just have to deal with it". Do you blame yourself or see it as something that happens to people who are living?

Negative self- talk is so damaging. Criticism, complaining, putting oneself down is all detrimental to your health. Of course we need to take blame when we are responsible. But you will get much farther in life looking at the glass half full instead of half empty.

So many negative influences attack us as we grow up. Many stick around even once we are grown. Friends who hate your success. Teachers who call you stupid (it is said Albert Einstein was once called unable to learn by one of his teachers). Spouses who don't see your potential.

Tell yourself that you are dynamic, powerful and able to accomplish anything you put your mind to. You can become the person you want to be.

You Have Greatness Inside of You

You have greatness inside of you. People who have achieved great things in this life did so because at some point in their life they believed it was possible. They reached inside and found the courage to dare to do great things. They won.

It is very hard to achieve greatness when you are unable to envision yourself being great. If you want to find out what you are truly capable of you need to look past the limitations of your life and see the endless possibilities that exist when you believe.

Look at the inventions we have before us that at one time were only a dream;

1) Traveling from one continent to the next would take weeks on a boat. Now an airplane can do it in hours. A boat was a great idea for traveling on water. But airplanes travel in the air. Someone with greatness inside of them had to come up with that idea first.

2) People use to use horses to get around. Now we use cars. Walking has its benefits but you can only go so far on foot. Horses allowed people to get places faster. But cars move even faster. Someone with greatness inside of them came up with that idea.

3) We used paper and pencil to keep notes. Now we use computers. Man has been writing for centuries. But now we use computers. They have replaced the need to depend strictly on paper and pencil. Instead we do more with computers than we ever had before. They allow us to collect and analyze more data than we could have dreamed possible. This is the result of someone having an idea that such a concept would be possible.

4) We looked at the moon. Now we have walked on it. Surveyed it. The moon is over 250,000 miles away and people have dreamed about space travel. Yet some added feet to the dream and we went from looking at the moon to walking on it. Someone with greatness inside of them came up with that idea.

I could go through so many other inventions (the toilet, cellphone, television, microwave, toaster, etc.) and the one thing all of these items have in common is that someone with greatness inside of them came up with the idea. The world has been benefiting from this and continues to benefit.

Don't cheat the world of your contribution to things being better for us all. We need your greatness to come out.

Live a Life That Matters

If you are alive today then you have two choices; you can live a life that has no real substance or you can live a life that matters. What's the difference?

To get up every day, go to work, come home, relax, spend time with family and loved ones only to go to bed and repeat that cycle every day is not a fulfilling life. Yes, it is functional. It may even pay the bills. But your life is about much more than just paying the bills.

What about a life where you still get up, go to work and come home to relax with family and friends but to find more than that. To discover that there are hurting people all around us who can use a hand up instead of a handout. To inspire, encourage and enable people to get back up again. To go to bed each night feeling like your contribution to someone else's life has made a difference is a great way to end the day.

No matter what accomplishments you may be able to do in your lifetime, the things that will have the longest lasting effect are the things you do that impact another person's life in a positive way. To feed the hungry when you are able to eat each day and make that happen for others is great; to clothe the naked when your closet is full of clothes is fulfilling. To visit the sick, comfort the lonely and show compassion to the hurting gives you that warm, fuzzy feeling in your heart.

What matters most to you? What encourages you each day to get up and keep on keeping on? What offers you the most fulfillment? Do you realize that you were put here on this earth for a reason? Every life, no matter how insignificant, matters. Actually there are no insignificant lives. Some of us may do things that warrant more attention, make more money or end up in the public eye. But a mother who cares for her children has a significant life. A father who cares for his sick parents has a significant life. A teacher who impacts the lives of her students has a life that matters. No matter where a person is in life, if they make someone else's life better, they are doing something that matters.

Live for more than yourself. Make the lives of others better because you are alive.

Give Your Attitude a Needed Adjustment

People can spend a lot of time complaining. We complain about what has gone wrong, what is currently going wrong and what will be wrong tomorrow. We see the problems in every situation and focus on what is wrong so much it's hard to see anything going right.

This perception causes our attitude to become blurred. Negativity is contagious and it starts with perception. Do you see the cup half full or half empty? Do you see the good in every bad situation or the bad in every good one? It is easy to think that our problems are our problem but every problem has a solution. The real problem is allowing our attitude to get so sour that we cannot believe there is a light at the end of the tunnel.

I want to encourage you to adopt a new attitude. A positive attitude stemming from looking at the things in your situation that are still good. Focus on what is going right because there is always hope in the midst of every storm.

In the movie GRAVITY Sandra Bullock plays a scientist who is trapped in space. In the beginning of the movie she talks and feels hopeless. She is in space, alone with no means of communicating to Earth. She has lost her companion who was helping her do her job in space. It appears that she will just give up and die.

George Clooney plays her companion. He encourages her (before he dies) that she must believe she can get to the other space station and catch a ride back to earth. He shares with her ideas as to how to make that happen.

In the movie there is a scene where she starts to tell herself she can do it. And she proceeds to try. Does she face difficulties? Yes. Is it hard? Yes. But what I noticed is that the moment her attitude changed, she did. Her situation was still bleak and wrought with many obstacles. But she consistently plowed through them until she reached her goal.

I know a lot of books have been written on attitude. And there is a definite place to learn as much about how your attitude impacts the altitude you will soar to in your life. I encourage you to think about the situation you are facing, see that it too will pass and get your attitude rooted in positive thinking.

Stop Complaining

If you have never complained before, disregard this chapter. If not, then this is for you.

There is a story in the Bible about a man who was crippled and his friends bought him to Jesus. We don't know how long he had been crippled but it took 4 men to carry him. As Jesus saw him he said to him "rise, take up your bed and walk." This advice still rings true over 2000 years from when it was first spoken.

All of us have problems. Many times these problems no only knock us down, they take us out. While we are lying there on our back unable to see what is going to happen yet the tendency is to do the "human" thing; complain. We speak ill of our circumstances, of people, of our lives.

If you are not careful you can stay on your back and complain your entire life away. Looking at what you don't have, can't do or are unable to accomplish. But what will that do for you? Will it give you hope? Will it make you smile?

No!!!

How about this; how about instead of all the complaining, we did the following;

1) *Stop complaining* - too many people view their life as a completed book instead of as a chapter in a book that is still being written. Stop talking about what is and begin to speak what could be.

In baseball, if you bat over.300 you are considered a good ball player. Some of the best players to ever play the game never achieved a.400. But when you think about it, a good ball player connects 3 out of ten times when he is at back. He strikes out or fails to hit the ball 70% of the time. Yet he is considered good and no player really maintains a.400.

In life it's not how many times you strike out. It's all about how many swings you continue to take. One home run can erase 2 strikes any game you play in.

2) *Get up* - once you stop complaining, stand. Get up to your feet. Get off your back. Stop lying down as if you have no choice. Of course you have a choice. You can get up and look around. It's possible. Just do it.

Even a baby knows "I will never walk if I am unwilling to stand up."

3) *Walk* - take a step. Go for it. Yes, you can do it. Tell yourself that even if no one else does. You can do it.

Your Gifts Will Make Room For You

Your gifts will make room for you. They will usher you into the presence of great men and women. They will make you known in the world you live in. And this will ultimately make life not only more enjoyable but memorable as well.

Each of us has been given a set of gifts. My gifts are not your gifts. My gifts belong to me and are for me. Your gifts belong to you and are for you alone. These gifts make us special when compared to everyone else we come in contact with.

Why do we each have gifts? Because we are all unique individuals. We have been blessed to enjoy so many wonderful talents that when we learn how to use them, they can take us to some incredible places. They open doors of opportunities for us to things we have never seen.

Let me offer you some information about your gifts and how they can make the life you live very special.

1) *You are special* - there is no one else in the world quite like you. Some people resemble you but they are not you. They may sound like you, laugh like you and even cry like you. But they are not you. When you were created the mold was broken. Even identical twins realize as they get older that although they have a lot in common, they are still two distinct individuals.

We are special because we are so different. We live our lives as individuals and do what we feel we should be doing when we feel we should be doing it.

2) *You are gifted.* The talents and abilities we have shape our personalities. Maybe it's singing (look at the many beautiful voices we enjoy but the singers we listen to). It could be painting (as when we visit a museum or an art gallery). Cooking. Swimming. Dancing. Playing musical instruments. The list goes on and on. It is learning what these gifts are that we possess and how to best use them that holds the door to our future success.

3) *You are cool.* Many times as we get older we feel like we have just had it. We can no longer related to the communities that surround us. We are out of touch with today's reality. That is so far from the truth. Even if you are not as hip as some, cool is still in you.

4) *You are a winner* - Winning is in you. Getting to the top of your endeavors and making strides in your career goals should be everyone's goal. The way to get to the top is to achieve on a high level utilizing the gifts you have.

You Can Fix Your Life

Life is not fair. Sad statement but true nevertheless. We would love to think that everyone starts off on the same page and has the same opportunities but it's not like that. Some of us do start way behind the starting line.

There is no way to discount obvious advantages. If you had the privilege of growing up in a home with 2 loving parents who nurtured you, cared for you and showed you unconditional love, then you begin life from the perspective of "universal acceptance." In your world, you found acceptance early. Your self- esteem has a great chance of being strong.

But think about all the people who did not grow up with those advantages. Maybe you didn't have 2 accepting parents. Maybe you didn't even have one. Instead of finding love, your earlier experiences with childhood may be filled with rejection, separation and even isolation. Your self- esteem has been attacked and you could feel a lot of hurt.

Sometimes people say that growing up in these two different situations don't make a difference. You live in the land of opportunity. You can be whatever you set your mind to. Those statements are true but they fail to take into account the position one is in when their past is so marred with disappointment.

You can fix it! You can still turn lemons into lemonade and enjoy a full life. Your past does not have to dictate your future. The answer to your future happiness lies within you. Let me share with you why I am saying this;

1) *How do you view your past*- Thomas Edison failed over 1000 times in his efforts to create a light bulb. Yet when asked about these failures his response was "I found 1000 ways it will not work. That's progress". Remember, it is not what happens to you that determines your future; it is how you choose to interpret those events.

2) *What do you say about your past* - do you talk about all the people who didn't do right by you or do you focus on those did? Maybe mom or dad wasn't there but grandma and grandpa was. Maybe your spouse was unfaithful but you have a friend who stuck by you closer than a brother. Look to focus on the good and speak good things about it.

3) *What does your future look like*- do you see gloom and doom? Do you see thunderstorms, tornadoes and earthquakes ahead? Or do you see darkness today but know the sun is coming out in the morning? Yes, it is hard today but it is not permanent. Even bad days are temporary.

You can fix it! Don't quit. And never, ever, give up.

The Laws of Wealth Work for All – Part 1

Ever wonder why "the rich continue to get richer and the poorer keep on getting poorer?" Why some people seem to come into abundant living with relative ease while others struggle and strive their whole lives and never seem to quite enter in?

I have. And because of the things that happened to me in the past I was prompted to look into what was going on with my finances.

We all have heard the story of go to school, get your degree, get a job, work, retire and live happily ever after. But as the last few years have taught us this is a fairy tale. There is no guarantees in this life so even if we do these things, we can still end up miserable.

I want to share with you what I have found in my journey to increase my personal wealth. I hope these principles from the Laws of Wealth will help you as well;

1) *Understand that accumulating wealth is intentional, not an accident* - Consider the farmer who goes out into the spring and looks at his fields. He understands that in order to have a great harvest in the fall it will all depend on what he does in the spring. A good saying to remember when it comes to accumulating wealth is to take the advice of a wise farmer; "in the spring, you sow; in the summer you grow; in the fall you reap so that in the winter you can eat." This principles applies to those of us who want to accumulate wealth. There must be intentional and purpose for accumulation to occur.

2) *Understand wealth is a mentality not known to the poor* - people who accumulate wealth think a certain way and those who don't think that way seldom if ever accumulate. The goal to tapping into wealth accumulation is to change how we think about money and money shortage.

Wealthy people think in terms of abundance. They don't see the cup as half full. They don't believe we have shortages or that there is not enough. To them they will always have all they need and more. They know the world is full of resources.

We hear about energy shortages, gas shortages, oil shortages, etc. But the truth is there is more than we could ever use. It's been said that one hour of sunlight hits the earth with enough energy to power our world for a year. Abundance. The way of the wealthy.

The rest of the world tends to think in terms of shortage. Whenever something happens in the economy the first thought is "we don't have enough, we won't have enough. We are poor and will be poor because this is how it is and how it will be".

To get past the problems that scarcity and poverty provides, we must focus on the fact that this world is full of opportunities and blessings. Wealthy people go out and get because they expect to have. They refuse to see there is not enough. That is a lie.

You should believe the same.

The Laws of Wealth Work for Everyone – Part 2

We began this series of articles talking about the Laws of Wealth. These laws exist and those who accumulate large sums of wealth have not only learned these laws but apply them consistently to their every business and investing lives.

We look at the mentality of the wealthy. Today I want to explore the concept of "learn to pay yourself first". I suggest 10% of what you take home. If you can't start there then start somewhere. Even 1% beats 0%.

This seems like a pretty straightforward concept but sadly, most people do not adhere to this principle. I know I didn't for years. The reason was real simple; I barely had enough to cover my expenses. I certainly couldn't put any money aside.

Let me show you what I have learned about this principle. For starters, when you get paid and pay your bills you are paying your creditors. But when you fail to pay yourself you fail to pay your biggest creditor; you.

Why would I say that? Because you owe yourself for all the success and happiness you have had up to this point in your life. Thank God for electricity, food, a place to live, a car to drive, etc. But take you out of the picture and none of that would matters. You are indeed the most important component for your own life.

Look at this concepts I have learned about paying yourself first;

1) *You take care of you first* - this means that no matter what you owe, how much you owe and what you pay out, you know that number one has been taken care of. This gives us a sense of satisfaction knowing we didn't just work the last week for someone else.

2) *You can decide on what to do with your money* - when you earn money you also have to both spend and invest it. I find that the money I pay myself brings me the most satisfaction when I get to save and invest. This is great when you begin to get really excited about building your own portfolio.

3) *You can buy yourself your own reward* - I remember times when the only thing I wanted for the week was to get a haircut, maybe a massage or pedicure/manicure. Just wanted to pamper myself for a hard work. When you work hard (and I suggest you do that with all your heart if you are not doing that already) you deserve to play just as hard. Different people need different things so you need to see what you want and need. Then on occasion do that.

Pay yourself first. Reward yourself for all of your hard work. Then you won't need others to do that for you. And you will feel so much better.

These laws exist and those who accumulate large sums of wealth have not only learned these laws but apply them consistently to their business and investing lives.

The Laws of Wealth Work for Everyone – Part 3

Wealth is gotten on purpose. It can happen by accident, as when you just happen to buy the next hot stock before it explodes but those situations are not common. For the most part people accumulate wealth through following certain laws and adhering to certain mindsets.

Today I want to talk to you about putting the laws of savings and investing to work for you. Let us begin by exploring what the difference is between the two;

Savings - this is money you put up for the rainy day. It's where you keep your emergency fund or savings to pay for the new tires you want to purchase. Savings accounts typically follow these guidelines;

1) *Money is easily accessible* - you can get to it with relative ease

2) *Money is penalty free* - you don't get penalized for using the money when you need it

3) *Is not the place you look for great growth* - these accounts tend to get low or no interest and are not the place you put money you hope to grow.

We can place savings into checking, savings or money market accounts for easy access.

Investing - this is money you put aside for your future. It's where you place money that you are not going to need anytime soon. You watch this money to see its growth and to monitor its progress.

1) *Money invested is not easily accessible.* - Since this money is not meant to be spent it is placed in accounts that make it hard to just go and get your hands on.

2) *Rate of return is very important* - Here the interest rate earned and growth potential of your investment is paramount. When you are investing the rate of return is one of the key factors to determine whether or not it's a good investment.

3) *Diversity helps out* - there is an old saying "don't put all of your eggs in one basket." You want to spread your investment out over a few different vehicles to help offset investment risk. If all of your money was tied into one stock that fell (such as Enron) you could see your life savings dissolved in front of your eyes.

4) *Investing with knowledge of the investment is key*- Know whatever vehicle you are using as well as you can. This will prevent being surprised by changes in the market you don't understand. The easiest way to lose money is to not understand how an investment makes you money.

Sources here include CD's, Annuities, Stocks, Bonds and Real Estate which are not liquid investments. To accumulate real wealth, you must save and invest.

The Laws of Wealth Work for Everyone – Part 4

We have looked at different aspects of the Laws of Wealth. These laws work for everyone who will apply them and they can turn a mediocre life into one that has more success than anyone could have dreamed possible.

I want to pick up on the 4th law which is one where people have the greatest amount of control and yet so few take advantage of it; Invest heavily in yourself. Gain skills and knowledge that will propel your financial life to new levels.

Regardless of what vehicles you choose to drive your wealth upwards, you will need specialized knowledge in order to get there. Let me offer you some real life examples of how I have applied this principle to my own life.

Back in my 20's I wanted to purchase a house to live in. I was looking for a job and a friend suggested I get into mortgage lending. I got hires to work as a loan officer for a mortgage company. I worked in this field for 4 years and helped many people purchase their own home. When I was ready I put in an offer with one of the real estate agents I worked with and had a deal on my own house.

That deal proved to be very stressful. Me and my wife both worked, had good jobs and qualified for financing (which I knew because I was a loan officer). But the lender kept giving us delays. These delays stretched into 4 months which is unheard of in a traditional purchase.

The sellers of the house got so fed up they put the house back on the market and refused to give us an extension. I went to the lender and had a knock down drag out fight over the reasons it was taking them so long to fund. Then I went to the sellers and told them the house was mine and they could take the sign down. They were irate but I told them I had worked too hard for this house to just let the deal fail.

We did close. It was my specialized knowledge in how mortgage financing worked that helped me to prevail. I didn't know when I took the job I would need to go through what I did but I was happy I had the skills to make it so.

Get the knowledge you need to do the investing you want to. It will equip you to both acquire and face obstacles that will come as a result of you being in the world of investing.

The Laws of Wealth Work for Everyone – Part 5

I think the hardest part of dealing with growing personal wealth in today's economy is to have examples that relate to people wherever they are in their financial journey. Some people are just starting out. Others have gotten sidetracked through financial adversities and setbacks. Others are doing fine and just want to do better.

The next law of wealth I want to share with you is this; Invest in solid business opportunities you understand. Avoid get rich quick and pyramid schemes.

We know that to invest is to take our money and put it into a vehicle that has the hope of appreciation. We looked at a few such vehicles (stocks, real estate, etc.). What I want to look at is investing into a business concern.

Here are some pointers as you look into this facet of building lasting wealth;

1) *Business owners have a great chance of becoming an investor with solid returns* - when you own a business you have the choice of investing profits back into your business or investing them into another business. Either way it can be a win-win situation if that business does well.

2) *Ownership can be hands on, hands off or control through stock ownership* - do you want to own a restaurant where you also are the cook? Do you want to hire a General Manager who oversees the restaurant and you oversee him? Or do you want to purchase a restaurant gaining control through stock ownership? Many choices are available to the wise business owner.

3) *Remember, it is impossible to truly become wealthy without equity* - ownership is wealth. Period. Those who own nothing have nothing. It's like living your life but never having anything of your own. Develop an "I must own" mentality and thrive.

4) *Invest only in businesses you understand* - this is key. I have invested through the years in real estate companies and my knowledge of the field has saved me some major headaches. Because I understand the language, I know what to look for in a good investment and I understand how to turn a profit. I have explored other businesses I have an interest in and the advice for others has always been the same; "why do you want to invest in that? You don't understand it." It's no secret that when we don't understand we can potentially lose everything we have invested.

5) *Finally, avoid get rich quick schemes and pyramid schemes* - there is no such thing as quick wealth unless you engage in illegal activities. And any business that cannot grow unless you find other people to give you money is not a business. You must have either a product or service to sell in order to be considered a business.

The Laws of Wealth Work for Everyone – Part 6

As I have looked at these Laws of Wealth for my own life I have found them to be refreshing and satisfying. But of all the laws I have shared with you up till now this one is the one that has clearly caused me the most trouble. The law is simple; "avoid debt; poor people pay interest while rich people earn it".

I started out my life by focusing on the things so many young people do; I got a job, was going to school and wanted to get my first car. From the time I bought that car until many years later I was caught up in the web of debt. This web is woven in deceit and makes you feel like you are prospering when in reality you are not.

Let me share some history into this journey of mine and hopefully you can take a few nuggets of truth with you so as to not repeat these mistakes;

1) *No responsible adult educated me about debt prior to me getting into it* - my mother and father lived very simple lives and bought very few items on credit. They never owned a credit card and saved until they could afford to pay cash. When I was a teenager wanting my first car I had a job and could afford a note. Instead of talking to me about the pros and cons of debt they let me get in way over my head. My first car was through a loan shark who charged me over 20% interest even though I was not a bad credit risk. After 3 years of paying my car note and wanting to pay it off I found I still owed over 80% of the original sales price. Needless to say I was devastated.

2) *No one ever told me credit was not cash* - I was elated to get my first credit card and could not believe how easy it was to buy things. Then I kept getting more offers in the mail and just added to my growing credit card collection. Now, there is nothing wrong with credit cards. But if you max them out and then just move on to the next one, you are not growing financially. Then I was only making minimum payments on 10 credit cards and they were all maxed to the limit. Sad thing is, I used them mainly for stuff I didn't need and hardly ever used.

3) *No one ever told me cash is always king* - I felt that as long as I had credit, I was better than the guy with cash. It wasn't until I started missing out on opportunities because I was "overextended" did it begin to dawn on me; I had too much debt. Cash never worries about being overextended.

4) *It takes much longer to come out from under financial burdens than to get into them-* years. I am talking years to pay off debt, straighten out your credit, and increase your credit score. It takes discipline, hard work and a refusal to be a slave to debt any longer.

The Laws of Wealth Work for Everyone – Part 7

These laws of wealth we have been looking at are both time tested and true. For the serious investor who follows them they will allow you to accumulate wealth over your lifetime that can last well into retirement.

Today I want to address the idea of protecting the wealth you have. If you concentrate solely on making money and not on preservation of wealth, you would conceivably lose the wealth you have accumulated thus far.

I want to give you a word to the wise today; diversification. In order to best protect your wealth, diversify, diversify, and diversify.

What do I mean? Don't put all of your eggs into one basket. No matter how well you understand an investment you need to apply the principle of diversification. Let me explain with a few examples;

1) *Stocks* - Try to look at stocks in various sectors (technology, financial, housing, health, etc.). Then look for various companies in that same sector so that you can purchase shares in a variety of companies. Would you rather have 100% of your stocks invested in 1 stock or 10? Not only will diversification shield you better against market fluctuations but you can offset your overall risk by not being 100% in any one sector at any given time. Very hard for all sectors to be doing badly at the same time.

2) *Real Estate* - I have owned many different types of properties (single family homes, multiple unit dwellings, apartment buildings and office complexes. Each type of property is different and offers benefits to its owners. Yet single family homes are the best investments to have when you need to liquidate (easiest real estate to sell), apartment buildings are great for building a salary for yourself (due to many expenses being contained in one site as opposed to many buildings) and office complexes offer the best way to pass on building expenses to your tenants. Having a mixture of these types of properties in your portfolio can make your investments more solid.

3) *Businesses* - If you own a restaurant you may also have a catering business. Sometimes the best way to diversify is to add on other services to your already existent business model.

4) *Insurance* - There are many types of insurance to cover many different types of situations. Share the risks by having homeowners, auto, life and business insurance.

Invest wisely in your financial future.

The Laws of Wealth Work for Everyone – Part 8

This journey we have taken looking through the Laws of Wealth would be remiss without adding this final piece to the puzzle; with wealth comes the responsibility of giving back to the less fortunate.

I find that there are two types of wealth people. Many billionaires today (Bill Gates, Warren Buffet to name a few) have already made it known how they want to use their wealth to help those less fortunate. There are many other rich people who feel the same way.

Then you have those who will not give back. They accumulate great sums of wealth to lavish on themselves and their loved ones. When it comes to doing something great for others, they can never find the time to make it happen.

I hope that doesn't happen to you. I believe that every person has a responsibility to their fellow man. I live in Southern California and almost daily I am stopped by someone at a gas station, mall or grocery store seeking aid. Instead of being aggravated that they are "bothering" me I remind myself that I am blessed to have a life that has not put me in their place. Then I feel a responsibility to give back to them as I can.

Here are some principles to keep in mind when dealing with the less fortunate;

1) *Don't be condescending* - You never know how someone ended up needing help. Don't make the mistake of thinking people are just losers and need to help themselves. I have seen husbands pass away and a wife with children lose everything through no fault of their own. Treat the less fortunate with respect.

2) *Compassion goes a long way* - Let compassion flow out of you like a river. People love to see you care as they see that you do care.

3) *Use your wealth to help someone who can't help you back*- Give with no expectation of return from those you help. I believe that as we give it comes back to us, just not from the person we have helped.

4) *Be grateful, always* - This goes without saying. The one thing we all can flood the world with is gratitude. Be thankful for your education, accomplishments, family and the wealth you have accumulated in your lifetime. Let the world know that you know you made it because you worked hard and found help along the way. Remember, except for some advantages we had to get where we are today it could be use in need of a hand up.

There is no success found in solitude. Help others benefit from the wealth you acquire.

The Laws of Wealth Work for Everyone – Part 9

The Laws of Wealth are like the laws of science; they don't change so in order to benefit the most from them we have to learn what they are.

These laws cover our mental attitude, our willingness to share our wealth with the less fortunate, our skill at investing for a return and in this article, the need to find success through failure.

You will learn more about success in times of distress than in times of prosperity. Most lottery winners end up broke after a few years, regardless of how much money they won. Why? Unless you are mentally prepared to succeed, failure will be lurking around the door waiting to take you down.

As we have spoken about wealth we have to look at the price for failing. Many people consider failing to be a step in the wrong direction but failing when it comes to wealth accumulation can be a blessing. Why? Because in failure we learn what not to do in order to succeed.

Consider the following men who have failed and yet ultimately succeeded:

Henry Ford went bankrupt at the age of 40
Donald Trump was bankrupt at 44
Walt Disney went bankrupt in 1921
H.J, Heinz went bankrupt at the age of 31
Milton Hershey went bankrupt at the age of 23
Larry King went bankrupt at the age of 45
P. T. Barnum went bankrupt at the age of 46

These men became millionaires and billionaires. Each of these men are known for their accomplishments. Yet the failure they experienced have helped them to still be remembered in our day. In our failure we can find the answers that so eloquently elude us when we are successful.

I have seen failure up close and personal. I knew a man personally who endured the following;

He was a real estate investor who lost his properties (17 units) during economic crash
He lost his home and a commercial building he owned shortly thereafter
He had 3 different automobiles repossessed at different times of his life
His credit score fell to 440
He lost all his credit cards
He lost his wife of 30 years

In all of these situations these people faced insurmountable financial odds and yet prospered. How? By using failure as a stepping stone to future success.

Wealth is meant to grow due to being properly applied. And failure helps us to do what we need to in order to make it big.

How to Not Blow It in Business

Being in business can be a great thing. It can afford you the opportunity to not only work for yourself but to accumulate wealth and riches you may never see working on a job. As we look at the ways to build personal wealth consider owning your own business.

Contrary to popular belief we all work for ourselves and are our own corporation. Although over 80% of the people who work in this country get a check from an employer the truth is if you cannot accept the fact that you really work for yourself, you miss the whole point of living in a capitalistic country.

When you see yourself as a businessperson you begin to think about things like cash flow, expenses, income, ways to increase your income and decrease your expenses, to name a few. One of the main objectives of a business is to earn a profit. One of your main concerns should be having more money left over each month than more month than there is money.

If we look at what has been happening in the world of business the last 15 years we see people who were in business and blew it. Some ran billion dollar companies yet in the end the company was shut down, thousands lost their jobs and many investors were wiped out.

Here are some guidelines of things to not do if you want to remain in business;

1) *Always remember how you got there in the first place* - a lot of businesses are the result of sacrifice, blood, sweat and many tears. Once you get some success it helps to remember that your present success came from past sacrifices. This helps to keep you humble moving forward and watching your business prosper. Everyone who is anyone started somewhere.

2) *Staff according to your weaknesses, not your strengths* - no CEO can do it all. The things you excel at won't require someone else to do when you can do it. You may be creative, technical in your approach, imaginative or practical. Know your strengths so that you can staff to what you are weak at. This ensures your organization covers a lot of ground.

Don't surround yourself with people like yourself because they are comfortable to be with or people who are your friends and need a job. People with different gifts than you will undoubtedly be unlike you in many ways.

3) *Stay true to your original intentions* - when a business starts the CEO does so with an idea. As your business grows you must beware of being involved in businesses that take you away from your core. Years ago Sears owned an Insurance company, real estate company, mortgage company, and investment banker. As they returned back to their core business of retail they divested themselves of all of these businesses that were not in line with their core business.

Can you diversify? Certainly. But stay true to your core business because that is the only reason you are in business.

4) *Watch your cash*- as your business earns more and more money, there will be many temptations to spend it. Resist the urge to splurge just because you can.

5) *Minimize debt obligations* - a lot of businesses grow through debt accumulation. Work to maintain an acceptable debt level that will not wreck your company should the market experience a downturn (remember the real estate market in 2007-2009)

You can build a successful business that endures the tough times if you plan it right.

Things Can Get Better

Do I sound like a broken record? I sure hope so. I strongly believe that you can have in life what you are willing to put into it.

Ever wonder why so many people go through life appearing to struggle in areas that other people seem to have no problems at all? Why do some struggle while others strive and become great?

A better quality of life is possible to all of us. Yet how can we focus on the events and actions necessary to make our dreams a reality? I believe it starts with understanding the following;

1) Whatever the mind can conceive and believe, it can achieve - this is the definition of perseverance. Our mind is a great place to birth new ideas. All of the many inventions we enjoy today (airplanes, space shuttles, automobiles, computers and iPods) are all the result of a mind conceiving an idea to make something happen that had never existed before. But it is not enough to conceive a great idea; you must believe it is possible to accomplish. When the odds are stacked against, when we don't have the resources we need to make it so, we believe. We believe against the odds. We focus on seeing what we believe and conceive coming to pass. That is achievement. All things are possible to the person who would dare to believe.

2) You deserve better - why can't things be better for you? Why is it your neighbors can live in nice houses, drive nice cars and experience some of the finer things in life while you struggle? Does that seem fair to you? Not to me. The quality of life you enjoy will be impacted by the environment you are in. To do better you must see better, receive better, embrace better and believe that better is for you as well.

3) You must go after what you want - sitting around and daydreaming about better days, brighter days and greater days ahead means more than looking up into the sky and imagining alone. When I come out of my front door I see a series of mountains in front of me. Each morning I take the time to look at this magnificent sight and imagine how great the mind that thought those mountains up must be. The deliberate, intricate details it would take to make such a mass is breathtaking. I look at those mountains and see that I too can have what I want if I will but possess the strength of character to go after it.

Don't settle for less than the absolute best life has to offer you.

You Deserve the Best Life Possible

Life is such a precious thing. It is the essence of being. We get the word "alive" from looking at a life.

How is your life going? Are you feeling good about yourself and the direction you are headed. Do you love yourself? Do you love life?

Or have you had a few hard times, hit a few bumps in the road? Are you discouraged because things have not been going as you planned?

Into every life a little rain must fall (although sometimes it feels like a monsoon). None of us can live without having a few things go wrong for us. It's not the things that go wrong that determine our quality of life; it's how we internalize what has happened to us and what we do about it.

When it is raining, do we stand around and complain or go get an umbrella? Do we rejoice in hardship (not FOR hardships but while we are IN them)? Do we see the cup as half empty or half full? Do we look for the good or focus on the bad?

I consider myself to be a pretty optimistic person. Yet I noticed that over the years as I have faced my own challenges, I spent more time talking about what is wrong, why it is wrong, where do I go from here instead of accepting the bad, looking for the good and making decisions that would ultimately lead me out of the mess.

I want to encourage you today to "live your life". Look for the good in every situation. See how you can turn lemons into lemonade, tragedy into triumph and losing into winning.

Here are a few tips on how to live your life;

1) With a dream - children are guilty of being big dreams. But as we grow up our dreams get crushed. We are told we cannot do something, should not do something, will not do something. Many have been called stupid and unrealistic for dreaming. Keep your dreams!

2) With great expectancy - get up each day and believe "the rest of my life will be the best of my life". Your best days are not behind you but ahead. See your future filled with hope and expectancy.

3) With hope - hope will get you up when you are sick. Hope will make you believe when the doctor says you are done. Hope will cause you to see farther than your eyes will allow. Helen Keller said "what is worse than no eyes is to have eyes with no vision".

What do you see for your life today? I hope you see the world is in front of your waiting for you to arrive and show up.

Financial Prosperity Now

There are some basic needs we all have as individuals that need to be met. At the top of the list are the needs necessary for survival - food, clothing, shelter. These basic needs can be met with ease when one has financial prosperity to meet those needs.

The focus is to be able to meet our daily needs. Jesus never went around with a lot of money (although he did have a treasurer. Broke people don't need treasurers). Yet he also knew that he would be able to meet every need that arose because he walked in financial prosperity. H knew how to meet needs once they arose.

Here are some ideas on what it means to walk in financial prosperity;

1) *Knowing that you can meet every need that comes up* - there are always enough resources to meet current needs. The fallacy is when we look at a need and believe there is no provision. In America we waste a ton of food each day. People eat at a restaurant and leave plenty of food on their plates. It's amazing how those who have resources tend to waste more than those who don't.

2) *Knowing that you have more than you will ever need at your disposal* - an abundance mentality is necessary to walk in financial prosperity. This mentality will create within us the assurance that we have all that we need whenever we need it. All we have to do is learn how to tap into this abundance which is all around us.

3) *Never thinking you are in lack but only in abundance* - it is very hard to think "I have abundant resources at my disposal." Yet that is exactly what we must think in order to achieve our goals. As a man thinks, so shall he be. We have to think that we can meet every need at every occasion if we hope to live that way.

4) *Never speaking lack but talking abundance* - just like we have to think abundance we have to speak it as well. Negative talk does not give us positive results. What you want to see happen in your life you must be willing to say it. The focus has to be on becoming what we envision and that includes being bold enough to say what we mean and mean what we say.

Financial Prosperity works for all who would believe in it.

The Price of Success is everything

People look to be successful in life. The typical expectation.is that we can and will be successful because we are willing to try hard. We work from sun up to sundown and we will be successful in all that we do.

Although many wish that would be true, the fact is that it is not. The price one must be willing to pay is everything. But it's not always what people think it is.

I have had the pleasure of being both employee and employer. In this capacity you get to sit on one side of the interview desk trying to convince someone else that you are a good fit for their company. On the other hand as an employer you get to try to access whether someone will be a good fit for your company. Most times people focus on the resume and past performance to determine potential success. I know I have and sadly, it seldom works.

Let me begin with sharing with you four common fallacies that result from thinking success can come through only hard work;

1) Don't believe that future success is measured by what you have done before. Although the past is an indication of what you have been able to do, it is not the best indication of what you will do in the future. We must gauge our future success by our present performance. What you do today with the opportunity you have before you will determine how far you go.

2) Any time you have fallen into a slump take the time to learn more about the business you are in so that you can reinvent the way you approach it and make adjustments. Change is inevitable for future success.

3) Impatience due to working somewhere and not experiencing immediate success does not mean you are in the profession or career. It can mean you will need time to improve yourself to function at the level you believe you are capable of.

4) If you focus too much on your problems, you won't see your solutions. Every problem has a way to be fixed. The key is staying focused on your end result so that you can see what that solution is. Most of the inventions we use today came about because a problem existed and people worked diligently to find a solution that worked. In time they did just that.

Jeff Davis is very aware of the pitfalls of not having money and the benefits of having more than you need. He says *"If you have to choose between not having enough or having more than you need, choose to have more. At least you can give to others who have needs."*

He is the President of The Lordship Companies Inc. a real estate investment company and insurance agency. Located in Southern California he works diligently to be able to both work hard and play hard.

He is the author of numerous books on the subjects of finances, real estate, sales, marriage and family. Visit Amazon and Createspace or one of his websites for more information.

www.thelordshipcompanies.com

www.drjeffwrites.com

www.ingramcontent.com/pod-product-compliance
Lightning Source LLC
Chambersburg PA
CBHW070802180526
45168CB00004B/1728